TEXAS

Past and Present

Jeanne Nagle

rosen publishing's
rosen central

New York

*To Matt and Emily, whose kind gifts help me
remember the Alamo every time I cook*

Published in 2010 by The Rosen Publishing Group, Inc.
29 East 21st Street, New York, NY 10010

First Edition

Library of Congress Cataloging-in-Publication Data

Nagle, Jeanne M.
Texas: past and present / Jeanne Nagle.
    p. cm.—(The United States: past and present)
Includes bibliographical references and index.
ISBN-13: 978-1-4358-5287-7 (library binding)
ISBN-13: 978-1-4358-5572-4 (pbk)
ISBN-13: 978-1-4358-5573-1 (6 pack)
1. Texas—Juvenile literature. 2. Texas—History—Juvenile literature. I. Title.
F386.3.N34 2010
976.4—dc22

                                                                    2008050962

Manufactured in the United States of America

On the cover: Top left: An oil field photographed in 1917. Top right: An astronaut
trains at the Johnson Space Center. Bottom: The Houston Metro train system.

Contents

Introduction   5

Chapter 1
The Geography of Texas   6

Chapter 2
The History of Texas   13

Chapter 3
The Government of Texas   20

Chapter 4
The Economy of Texas   27

Chapter 5
**People from Texas:
Past and Present**   33

Timeline   39

Texas at a Glance   40

Glossary   42

For More Information   43

For Further Reading   44

Bibliography   45

Index   46

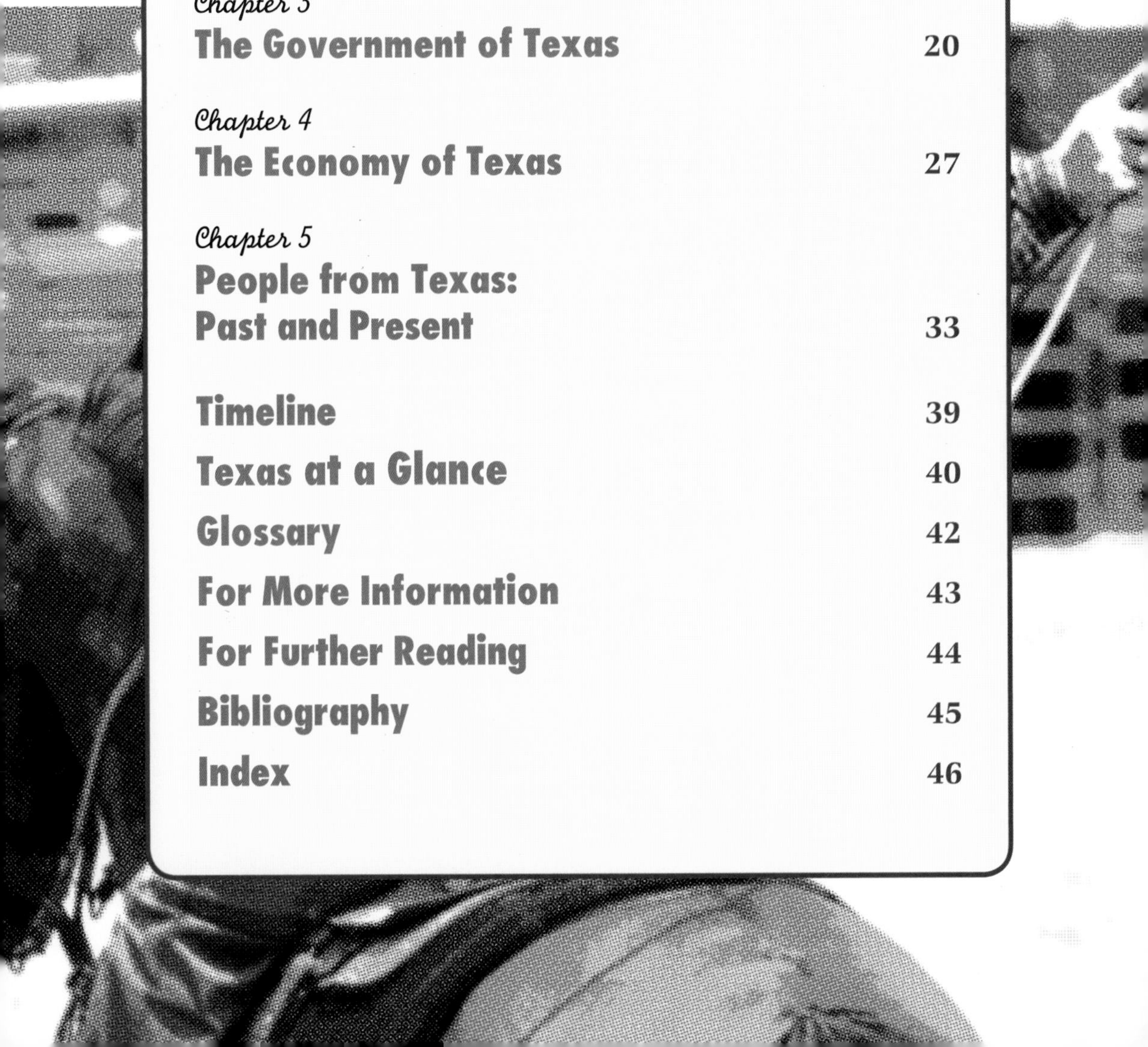

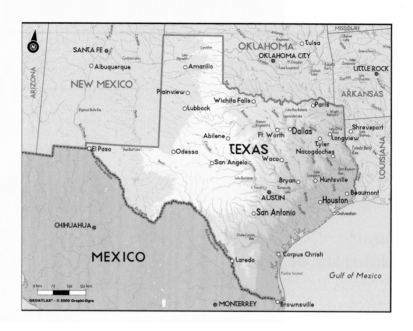

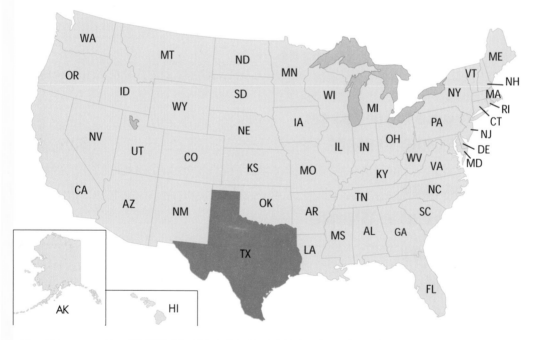

Among the largest states in the country, Texas has an extensive coastline, a border with Mexico, and a variety of landscapes that give rise to numerous industries.

Introduction

Texas has one of the most colorful pasts of any American state. Home to legendary pioneers, hard-living cowboys, and four U.S. presidents, Texas has, at one time or another, belonged to no less than four different countries. Technically, the count rises to five if you include an episode when the territory declared itself an independent republic. Wars have been fought over ownership of the land Texas occupies. Battles have also raged within the state's boundaries for causes as noble as independence and as shameful as the right to own slaves.

Texas has also seen its share of man-made and natural disasters. One of the country's most beloved presidents, John F. Kennedy, was assassinated in the city of Dallas, while Galveston was the site of a devastating hurricane that is considered the nation's deadliest natural disaster ever.

Present-day Texas is pretty interesting, too. Thriving industries and an astounding variety of landscapes are some of the qualities the state offers. As the largest producer of oil in the nation, Texas finds itself in the middle of discussions and controversy regarding energy and the use of fossil fuels. And then there is the spirit and unique outlook of Texans, who possess a sense of independence so strong, it makes residents proud of their state capital's "weird" reputation. Then as now, it is worth getting to know what Texas is all about.

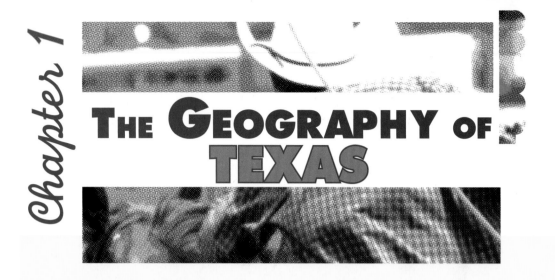

Chapter 1

The Geography of Texas

Because of its location within the United States, there has been a long-standing debate about whether Texas should be considered a southern state or a western state. Perhaps former senator William Blakely said it best when he declared, "Texas is neither southern or western. Texas is Texas."

One point everybody agrees on is that, geographically speaking, Texas is big. Maps of the United States show why. Located in the south-central portion of the nation, the state covers more than 775 miles (1,247 kilometers) from east to west and more than 800 miles (1,287 km) from north to south. A total of close to 269,000 square miles (696,706 sq km) of land make it the second-largest American state, after Alaska.

Land mass is not the state's only impressive geographic characteristic, however. In terms of the variety of terrain, significant bodies of water, and the population of its major cities, Texas is one super-sized state.

A Bit of Everything

Geographically, North America is a wonderful combination of towering mountain peaks and low-lying valleys, lush plains and arid deserts, shimmering coasts, shaded forests, and rolling hills. Because of its

Swamps and forests are common in the Piney Woods region of Texas. When the two meet, the resulting marshy area is called a slough.

size and location, Texas contains virtually every feature and landform that exists on the continent, with the exception of an icy tundra.

In order to examine the geography of Texas, it is helpful to break down the state into regions. To the east lies an area known as the Piney Woods. As the name suggests, there are pine forests in this region. Swamps are another common feature, including those found in the area's Big Thicket Nature Preserve. Hills and farmland also distinguish parts of the region.

The Prairies and Lakes region also has a self-explanatory name. While there are sparse forests along the region's eastern border with the Piney Woods, the area is predominantly filled with lakes and prairies, which are wide swathes of land without trees, just grass.

To the southeast is the Gulf Coast. Islands and marshes are abundant in the eastern half of the region, which lies along the Gulf of Mexico. Beaches are also plentiful. In fact, America's longest undeveloped beach, Padre Island National Seashore, is located in this section of Texas. Farther inland, to the west, the Gulf Coast region supports grassy plains.

The South Texas Plains cover the southernmost part of Texas. The section nearest the coast consists largely of sand, while there is rich farmland farther inland and brush—a dry, dusty area with scraggly trees and prickly bushes—near the border with Mexico.

Hill Country is what Texans call the state's central region. Grassy hills at the edge of the area turn into cliffs, canyons, and rock ledges near the region's middle. Many springs and underground lakes can be found among the area's rocks and sandy soil.

To the north of Hill Country is the Texas Panhandle. Great plains, which are flat expanses of grasslands or scrub as far as the eye can see, make up most of this region. However, deep canyons, cut into the plains by flowing rivers and streams, are common in the eastern and western portions.

Finally, there is the Big Bend region of west Texas. Miles of rugged mountains mingle with acres of sandy soil from the Chihuahuan Desert, the bulk of which is in Mexico. Because it is so dry and inhospitable, not many people live in this region.

Rivers and the Gulf

The Big Bend region is named after a curve in the Rio Grande, the longest river in Texas and one of about a dozen major rivers that flow

The fourth-longest river in the United States, the Rio Grande winds throughout west Texas. In Mexico, where the river also travels, it is known as Rio Bravo.

throughout the state. Add approximately 3,700 named streams and thousands of lakes and ponds, and it's easy to see how water covers nearly 200,000 miles (321,868 km) of the state.

A handful of Texas's rivers provide more than just fresh water for drinking and watering crops and livestock. Three waterways serve as natural boundaries that define the state's borders and give Texas its unique geographic shape. The Rio Grande, which is Spanish for "large river," acts as a border between Texas and Mexico in the western part of the state. To the northeast, Texas is separated from Louisiana by the Sabine River, while the Red River makes up a majority of the

Gulf Ports

The Gulf of Mexico has been a major U.S. port for hundreds of years and has been quite important to the Texas economy. But what's being shipped to and from other countries has changed over time.

In the 1800s, the chief exports shipped overseas from the Gulf were the mainstay crops of the South at the time: sugar and cotton. The Gulf Coast city of Galveston was the heartbeat of Texas shipping, becoming the third-busiest port in America by the end of the nineteenth century.

Winds of change were blowing in 1900—literally and figuratively. A hurricane destroyed Galveston that year, and the city never recovered its prominence as a shipping port. A year later, oil was discovered in the town of Beaumont, near Houston. Oil is now the main export of the Gulf Coast, and instead of Galveston, Houston is currently the third-largest port in the United States.

state's northern boundary with Oklahoma and a small part of the Texas–Oklahoma border.

The Red River flows into the Mississippi River, but the other two— like most major rivers in Texas—empty into the Gulf of Mexico. A gulf is a body of water formed when the ocean is partly enclosed by land. Mexico, the southeastern United States, and Cuba form a basin that holds water from the Atlantic Ocean, forming the Gulf of Mexico. Stretching across four states other than Texas (Louisiana, Alabama, Mississippi, and Florida) in the United States, the Gulf measures approximately 995 miles (1,600 km) in total from east to west. Only about 350 miles (563 km) stretch along the Texas coast.

Major Cities

Six of the top twenty-five U.S. cities with the largest populations are in Texas: Houston (number 4), San Antonio (7), Dallas (9), Austin (16), Fort Worth (17), and El Paso (21).

With a population estimated at around three million, Houston occupies 596 square miles (1,543 sq km) on the Gulf Coast. It is a busy port city also known for oil production and aeronautics. The Lyndon B. Johnson Space Center, which is the mission control center for National Aeronautics and Space Administration (NASA) has been in the city since it opened in 1963.

Vibrant colors, people mingling, and lights reflecting on the water give San Antonio's River Walk a festive atmosphere at night.

Nearly 1,329,000 people live in San Antonio, a community in the South Texas Plains region of the state. San Antonio is a favorite tourist destination, thanks to its River Walk, a beautiful and trendy pedestrian shopping district. The city is also the site of the Alamo, which was a famous fort and battleground during the Texas Revolution.

Dallas, a 343-square-mile (888 sq km) city located in the Prairies and Lakes region, is home to more than 1,200,000 people. Arguably the most well-known Texas city by people from other states, Dallas serves as the headquarters for several Fortune 500 companies. The population (702,850) of nearby Fort Worth is frequently combined with the populations of Dallas and the city of Arlington, creating the fourth-largest metropolitan area in the nation.

The state capital, Austin, is located on the banks of the Colorado River. The University of Texas built its main campus here. One of the state's leading business centers, Austin also has a fun and creative side. The city supports a thriving music industry and even bills itself as the "Live Music Capital of the World." The city's unofficial slogan is "Keep Austin Weird," which promotes small business entrepreneurship and a sense of free-spiritedness. Austin has a population of roughly 743,000.

Surrounded by the Franklin Mountains and the Rio Grande, El Paso is located in the far-west reaches of the Big Bend region. Texas's sixth-largest city is on the border with Mexico and very close to the neighboring state of New Mexico. Almost 610,000 people live in El Paso, which is especially impressive given that most of the area around the city is desert wilderness.

Chapter 2

The History of Texas

The history of Texas reaches back tens of thousands of years. Tools, weapons, and other artifacts unearthed throughout Texas suggest that the state has been occupied for quite some time. Paleoamericans are what scientists call the early inhabitants of North and South America, including the area that is now Texas.

After the Paleoamericans came Native Americans. In prehistoric times, Pueblo civilizations coexisted on the plains of what is modern-day Texas and New Mexico. Pueblos are the generic name given to a number of native cultures who have lived in the southwestern United States since 100 BCE. They were later joined by a number of native communities in west and east Texas, and along the Rio Grande. These tribes included the Caddo, an advanced culture with sophisticated farming and agricultural practices, and the Apache.

Exploration and Settlement

The arrival of European explorers in the 1500s brought big changes to the area. Spanish voyager Alonso Alvarez de Pineda was the first non-native to explore Texas, in 1519. Almost ten years later, sailor Alvar Núñez Cabeza de Vaca was shipwrecked on Galveston Island and captured by a group of natives. He went from being a slave of

Other Spaniards explored the region before him, but Francisco Vasquez de Coronado was the first to claim Texas land for his queen.

the natives to trading with them. Through his travels as a trader, he explored the area.

Another Spaniard, Francisco Vasquez de Coronado, claimed a parcel of western land near the Rio Grande in 1540, but it wasn't until 1716 that Spanish citizens settled in the area. By that time, Texas had become part of a Spanish empire in North America, along with California and Mexico. Texas was considered a part of Mexico at the time.

In the 1680s, the French also established an outpost in eastern Texas—by accident. While trying to set up a colony along the Mississippi River, an explorer named La Salle sailed too far and wound up 400 miles (644 km) off course to the west, along the Texas Gulf Coast. Eventually realizing his mistake, La Salle left hundreds of settlers behind in an unfinished fort and set off to find the Mississippi.

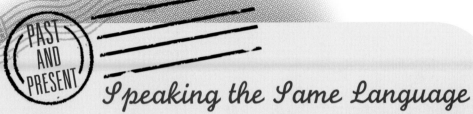

Speaking the Same Language

When Mexico had control over Texas, the ruling government created laws that protected the rights of its American settlers. Among these was the designation of English as the second official language of the state. The idea was to make American immigrants comfortable and feel accepted.

Compare that to what's happening today in Texas and other parts of the United States. A movement is under way to have English declared the official language of the United States. This is particularly controversial in states that have large populations of Mexican immigrants, such as Texas. While the state doesn't presently have an official language, recent polls have shown that 78 percent of Texans would vote in favor of legislation making English the official language.

Reaction has been mixed. One Texas town with a heavily Mexican population, El Cenizo, responded by declaring Spanish its official language.

When the Spanish found out that the French were living on their land, they sent search parties to find the fort and destroy it. Disease and attacks by animals and Indians had killed most of the settlers, so by the time the Spanish found it, the fort had already been abandoned. To keep the French away in the future, the Spanish created more settlements of their own in east Texas.

Trouble with Mexico

By the nineteenth century, the Spanish empire had begun to crumble. Mexico gained its independence from Spain in 1821 and was given control of Texas. Right before this, however, Spain had agreed to let Stephen Austin bring a group of American settlers into the territory.

Friction between American settlers and the Mexican government led to the bloody and famous battle at the Alamo.

The Mexican government let Austin's group and others stay, but in 1830, Mexico passed a law designed to keep U.S. citizens from emigrating to Texas.

Settlers ignored the law and moved to Texas in droves. Soon, more Americans lived in Texas than Mexicans. The colonists longed for independence from Mexico, and the U.S. government sought to annex the state, meaning to make it part of America. Mexico responded by enforcing immigration and taxation laws. Angry colonists, backed by Mexican residents called Tejanos, began the Texas Revolution in October 1835.

The most famous battle of the war for independence took place at the Alamo, an abandoned San Antonio mission that the colonists used as an army fort. On February 23, 1836, Mexican forces, led by President Santa Ana, attacked the Alamo. The battle lasted nearly two weeks and ended with a Mexican victory. Close to two hundred rebels died as a result, including famous pioneer Jim Bowie and Tennessee volunteer Davy Crockett.

Another important fight was the battle at San Jacinto, which took place six weeks after the colonists' defeat in San Antonio. With a war cry of "Remember the Alamo!" commander Sam Houston and the Texas Army defeated Mexican forces. In defeat, Santa Ana was forced to sign a treaty that gave Texas its independence.

Republic of Texas and Statehood

Some people joke that Texas is so large, it could be its own country. Actually, that's not too far from the truth. After winning its independence from Mexico, Texas declared itself a sovereign, or self-governing, nation. San Jacinto hero Sam Houston was elected president, and a congress was voted into office.

Despite enjoying their hard-won freedom, most Texans favored annexation, which meant joining the United States. At first, the American government was hesitant to make Texas a state. Representatives from northern U.S. states were especially against such a move because they were against slavery, and they didn't want to add another southern slave state to the Union. The prospect of gaining so much land proved too appealing, however, and Texas was made a state in 1845.

Slavery again became an issue during the American Civil War. As a southern state that permitted slavery, Texas sided with the

Disagreements between political parties about whether to annex Texas or not made great material for newspaper cartoonists of the day.

Confederacy and seceded or separated from the United States in 1861—a mere sixteen years after it had been admitted to statehood. Like the other secessionist states, Texas was readmitted to the Union when the war ended.

Into the Twentieth Century

Expansion in Texas continued after the war. Many new residents were from the Southeast, people trying to escape land and economies ruined by years of fighting and make a fresh start. Some became cowboys and ranchers, but many more worked the land as farmers.

Railroad service, which was building in Texas before the Civil War, grew by leaps and bounds in the 1870s and 1880s. In addition to transportation, railroads provided a way for Texas farmers to get crops to markets around their vast state and elsewhere in the United States. Because they were able to reach new markets and sell more, many farmers were able to expand their operations—provided they could find extra land that hadn't been purchased already by other settlers.

Another noteworthy event occurred at the turn of the century in a tiny southeast town called Beaumont. In 1901, Texas native Pattillo Higgins and his engineer, Anthony Lucas, tapped into a gusher of oil that, at its peak, produced millions of barrels a day. Crowds flocked to the area, hoping to strike it rich. The start of oil drilling was an important moment in Texas history, mainly because it would shape the state's future so dramatically.

Chapter 3

THE GOVERNMENT OF TEXAS

The early settlers of Texas banded together and began work on forming a provisional, or temporary, government even before the state had officially won its independence. The importance of proper governance, which means being governed, has never been lost on Texans.

The state experienced unique growing pains in its early years, which forced changes in its government. For example, certain levels of independence the state enjoyed as the Republic of Texas had to be changed after annexation to the United States. Texas had to shift from operating as its own country, with a strong sense of independence, to being part of a nation, which meant playing by that nation's already-established rules. Succession during the Civil War, then being readmitted to the United States after the conflict had ended, brought about other governmental upheavals.

By 1846, however, Texas had pretty much settled into a stable form of government. With few exceptions, the basic structure of the Texas state government has not changed much since that time.

The State Constitution

Adopted in 1876, the Texas State Constitution outlines the organization and authority of the branches of state government. This version was

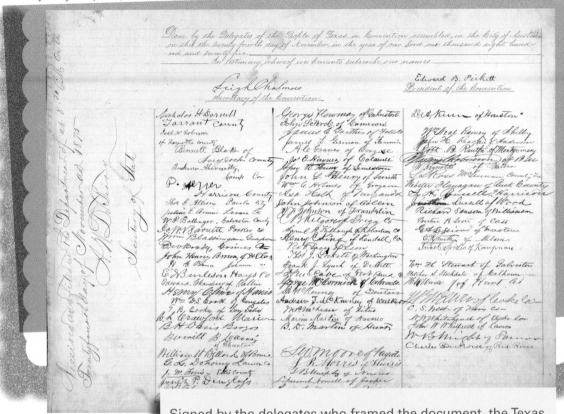

Signed by the delegates who framed the document, the Texas State Constitution is a long document, thanks to hundreds of amendments.

proposed after a hastily, and therefore poorly, constructed document written shortly before the state's readmission to the Union was judged unfit.

Like most other state constitutions, the Texas Constitution spells out in great detail the role and responsibilities of government at the state and local levels. Included are a Bill of Rights, specifics on how the government should operate, and the division of power among the executive, legislative, and judicial branches of

With its white pillars and two stories of tall windows, the Texas Governor's Mansion looks a little bit like the White House in Washington, D.C.

the state government. Certain policy issues, such as the funding of public education and tax collection, are also covered in the document.

The Texas Constitution was set up to reflect the time in which it was written, but things change. Economic and population growth have made some of the document's articles outdated. Changes that help modernize the constitution are accomplished through amendments. In Texas, an amendment must have the support of two-thirds of both the state senate and house of representatives to even be considered. Then, a majority of citizens must vote to ratify, or approve, the addition of the amendment to the constitution. Texas has the honor of being the state with the fourth-highest number of amendments to its constitution.

The Executive Branch

At the head of the Texas government is the governor. Normally, a governor has the ultimate say in matters of policy within his or her state. In Texas, though, the governor's power is limited or, more accurately, shared. The state operates under what's known as a plural executive branch, devised by the original framers, or writers, of the state constitution as a way to keep governors from becoming too powerful—a danger the original settlers had dealt with on more than one occasion.

A plural executive form of government means that day-to-day operations are overseen by several elected officials, not just the governor. Control over the state's legal system, budget, education, transportation, agriculture, public utilities, and land development fall under this system. Instead of a cabinet that supports the governor, there are individual political leaders who work for the people

Changing Parties

Prior to winning its independence and becoming a state, Texas was essentially a no-party state. Texans were in general agreement about the direction the state would take, and they had a common goal, which was to break free of Mexico. Politicians and statesmen didn't need to form political parties with different agendas.

After the Civil War, though, political disagreements became common. Two main parties took hold in the state: the liberal Radical Republicans and the more conservative Democrats. By the end of Reconstruction, which is what the time of rebuilding after the war was called, the Democrats had become the dominant party in Texas.

Today, however, Texas is considered a heavily Republican state. While this seems like a complete switch, it is actually more a change in name only. In the 1960s, the Democrats started leaning toward more liberal views, supporting causes like civil rights and increased state services. A majority of Texans have chosen to keep their conservative beliefs and backed the Republicans, who are now considered the more politically conservative party.

who elected them. Plural executive positions in Texas include lieutenant governor, attorney general, and comptroller, as well as hundreds of seats on various state boards and commissions.

What the governor of Texas does have control over is appointments to the constituencies with whom he or she shares power. An appointment is when someone is named to a specific political office. Chief among the Texas governor's appointments is the secretary of state, who mainly oversees the election process. The governor also directs, but doesn't control, the budget process and has control of the National Guard and limited say over police matters. He or she keeps the power of veto over the legislative branch, which lets the governor refuse the approval of bills and budget items.

The Justice System and the Legislature

The Texas state capitol houses the offices of the governor and other elected officials. Both houses of the legislature meet there.

The Texas state legislature is conventional in some ways, unconventional in others. On the traditional end, the legislature is divided into two houses, the senate and the house of representatives. Elected representatives from each house propose and pass legislation, or laws, designed to protect residents' health, welfare, and safety. What makes the Texas legislature different from just about every other state legislative body is that it is basically a part-time enterprise.

Texas legislators meet for regular sessions only 140 days every two years, starting in January of odd-numbered years. This is a special provision written into the state's constitution, aimed at reducing the impact of government interference on the fiercely independent state. Governmental business that is not handled in these biennial (once every two years) sessions is usually considered dead, although the governor has the option to call special legislative sessions if necessary.

The most powerful of the three branches of state government, the legislature also approves (or rejects) the governor's appointments, determines the fate of state agencies, and oversees government operations and budgets. Texas legislators do all that and pass hundreds of laws—all in a 140-day time frame.

Texas's judicial branch of government is like the justice systems of most American states—multilayered and complex. Many different courts—local, district, appellate, and supreme—hear and decide criminal and civil cases at the state level. The justice system is overseen by the state's attorney general, which is an elected position.

THE ECONOMY OF TEXAS

Texas's economy is as diverse as its regions and the people who live in each of them. In the Panhandle and west Texas are folks who make their living as ranchers. Lumber is big business in the eastern part of the state, throughout Piney Woods especially, and fishing and shipping bring in a great deal of money along the Gulf Coast. Farms and oil fields can be found practically everywhere within the state.

Texas has more Fortune 500 companies, which are the nation's top corporations, than any other American state. Measured by gross domestic product (GDP), which determines how much a country's goods and services are worth, the Texas economy is the fifteenth-most productive in the world.

Some types of businesses are big in certain cities only. For instance, aeronautics employs tens of thousands in Houston, home of the Johnson Space Center, but nowhere else in the state. Likewise, Dallas is considered a leader in the insurance sector of business. Following are the major industries found throughout the state.

The Power of "Black Gold"

Ever since 1901, when drilling began in earnest, the Texas economy has been dominated by oil exploration and processing. According to

Rows of oil tanks pop up across Texas, storing the thousands of gallons of "black gold" reserves produced by the state.

the state government–run TexasOne Web site, an overwhelming majority of the state's counties are involved in the production of crude oil, which is nicknamed "black gold." Oil and petroleum companies employ more than a quarter of a million Texas residents and add more than $60 billion to the state economy each year.

Oil is buried deep under the Texas soil and far beneath the Gulf of Mexico's waves. The areas of largest concentration are east Texas, which is where the original Texas oil boom began, and along the Gulf Coast. Estimated quantities of American oil available, called reserves, are the

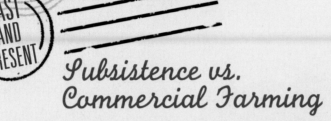

Subsistence vs. Commercial Farming

When Americans first started settling in Texas, they generally purchased enough land to build a house and do some farming. Known as subsistence farms, these small, family-owned plots of land ranged in size anywhere from 120 to 160 acres (48.5 to 64.75 hectares). They produced just enough crops to keep farmers and their families alive. (The word "subsist" means to maintain life or barely sufficient to sustain life.) Occasionally, farm families were able to sell extra products to local merchants or barter crops and livestock to purchase necessities like ground flour. Mostly, though, they simply ate what they raised.

Today, farms in Texas are mostly commercial enterprises. This is farming done on a large scale. Using technology and machinery to make production more efficient, today's Texas farmers are able to feed millions of people across the nation and around the world, not just their own families. These days, federal government subsidies, which are payments designed as an incentive to keep farming profitable, are readily available in the state as well.

highest in Texas. Only the federal government, which owns the rights to oil in regions off American shorelines, controls more reserves.

Deposits of natural gas and coal are also plentiful throughout the state. Texas is the largest producer of natural gas in the United States. One-third of the nation's total supply of natural gas is produced within the state each year. According to the U.S. Energy Information Administration, Texas is the fifth leading producer of coal in the nation. Pockets of bituminous coal are found in north-central and west Texas. Lignite, a lower-grade form of coal, exists underground in the east and central regions, with a broad band occurring across the state from the city of Laredo to the Louisiana border.

Golden grain and long-horned cattle are typical occupants of farms across the state. Cows and corn are the most profitable farm products in Texas.

Farming and Ranching

Agriculture is big business in Texas. The state's department of agriculture claims that about 80 percent of Texas land is used to grow crops or raise livestock. Texas is also America's third-largest exporter of agricultural products, which include meat, live animals, and crops used for food or livestock feed.

Without a doubt, cotton is the king of Texas crops. Researchers with the Texas A&M University Cotton Program estimate that Texans plant more than 6 million acres (2.43 hectares) of cotton every year.

Cotton production alone brings in millions of dollars to the Texas economy annually.

Corn, wheat, hay, and grain sorghum round out the top five crops grown in Texas. Rice, pecans, and sugarcane are also top moneymakers for the state. Though not considered food crops, nursery and greenhouse plants are also big sellers, ranking just under cotton as a hot Texas agricultural commodity.

On the ranching end, cattle rank the highest in the state. In fact, the sale of beef cattle brings in the most money of all agricultural products in Texas. According to the National Agricultural Statistics Service, there were approximately 149,000 cattle ranches in operation in 2007. No wonder Texas is the number-one producer of beef cattle in America. Other profitable livestock raised in Texas includes chickens, hogs, and sheep. Goats raised in the state have made Texas the top producer of mohair, a type of wool made from the animals' hair.

Manufacturing

Taking raw materials and making goods is what manufacturing is all about. A June 2008 report by *Manufacturers' News, Inc. (MNI)* indicates that more than twenty-four thousand manufacturers employ more than one million people in Texas. Those figures make Texas the second-largest manufacturing state in the nation, after California. Manufacturing facilities are generally located in the state's larger cities. In fact, Houston ranks first in the number of U.S. manufacturing jobs, and the city has more manufacturers within city limits than there are in the entire state of Oregon, according to the *MNI* report.

Industrial machinery and equipment make up the state's largest manufacturing sector. Food processing, which involves preparing crops to be mixed, cut, cooked, baked, canned, or frozen, employs

The Texas computer industry was "short-circuited" in the early 2000s. But today, technology employment in the state is on the rise.

hundreds of thousands of Texans each year. Electronics, particularly semiconductor and silicon processing, is the state's leading high-tech manufacturing segment. Texas high-tech manufacturers were hard hit during the recession that followed the technology bubble burst of 2001, but there are signs of a comeback. The number of computer and semiconductor manufacturing jobs in the state either remained steady or grew in 2007, said Advancing the Business of Technology, which is a trade group that was formerly known as the American Electronics Association.

Texas also has a strong reputation as a leading chemical manufacturer. Fertilizers, sulfuric acid, and petroleum-based additives and products like benzene and propylene are among the top chemicals manufactured in the state.

Chapter 5

PEOPLE FROM TEXAS: PAST AND PRESENT

Texas has the distinction of being the home of four U.S. presidents. Dwight Eisenhower and Lyndon Johnson were born there, while George H. W. Bush and George W. Bush made the state their home later in life. Of course, these distinguished gentlemen are not the only notable Texans. From the state's founding fathers to entertainers and sports figures, Texas is full of famous and interesting figures.

Early Leaders

The Texas state capital is named after Stephen Fuller Austin. His father, Moses Austin, was the first to receive permission to bring American settlers into Texas when it was under Spanish rule, but he died before he was able to establish a colony. On his deathbed, he asked Stephen to take over his "Texas Venture."

Stephen Austin had made a name for himself as a soldier, a land speculator, and an Arkansas circuit court judge before honoring his father's request. Under his guidance, settlers began to colonize land near the Colorado and Brazos rivers in 1821. When Mexico won its independence from Spain and took control of the state, Austin acted as an agent between the settlers and the Mexican government. He was in favor of Texas independence and was even jailed for that belief. Austin

A hero at the battle of San Jacinto, Sam Houston was an early celebrity. Before moving to Texas, he'd lived with Cherokee Indians in Tennessee.

led troops early in the Texas Revolution. After the war, he ran for president of the Republic of Texas in 1836, but he lost to another popular Texan— Sam Houston.

Supposedly Houston had tried to get settlers to calm down as talk of a revolution swirled through the state. Once the Alamo came under attack, he reconsidered. As head of the newly formed Texas Army, Houston led troops in the decisive battle at San Jacinto. He was elected as the first president of the Republic of Texas and also served as governor of the state. Houston is considered by many to be "the Father of Texas."

Actors and Actresses

Several of today's movie and television celebrities started their paths to stardom in Texas. Born in Terrell, Jamie Foxx began acting on the small screen in the television series *In Living Color*. He went on to star in his own sitcom, *The Jamie Foxx Show*, before jumping to movies with 1992's *Toys*. Other films he has appeared in include *Any Given*

Sunday, *Collateral*, and *Dreamgirls*. The second actor, and first black man, to be nominated for two Academy Awards in the same year, Foxx won for Best Actor in 2004 for the movie *Ray*.

Other actors and actresses that are from Texas include Matthew McConaughey, who was born in Uvalde and grew up in Longview. His acting credits sometimes take a backseat to his being named *People*'s "Sexiest Man Alive" in 2005, followed by making

Texas native Jamie Foxx was a star football quarterback in high school. These days, though, he's better known as an Academy Award–winning actor.

that magazine's list of "Hottest Bachelors" in 2006. Jennifer Love Hewitt, who grew up in Waco, began as a child actor in the Disney series *Kids Incorporated*. Currently, she stars in the CBS show *Ghost Whisperer*. Actress Eva Longoria Parker stars as one of the title characters in ABC's *Desperate Housewives*. Originally from Corpus Christie, Longoria Parker is married to Tony Parker, a guard for the four-time NBA champion San Antonio Spurs.

Musicians

Lake Jackson was the hometown of Selena Quintanilla-Perez, a singer known simply as Selena. Considered the Queen of Tejano music, Selena

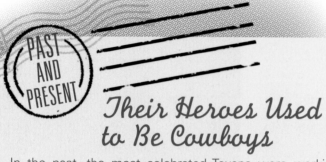

Their Heroes Used to Be Cowboys

In the past, the most celebrated Texans were working cowboys. There was Francisco Garcia, known for leading the first trail cattle drive in the state. Charles Goodnight was a Texas Ranger famous in his day for cross-breeding cattle to make them more appealing for commercial sale, saving the American buffalo from extinction, and founding a college. Civil War scout and frontier reporter John Baker Omohundro wrote about his cowboy adventures under the pen name Texas Jack. His articles, printed in the *New York Herald*, were practically required reading in the late 1800s.

Perhaps the most well-known Texas cowboy of old was Bill Pickett. He invented bulldogging, which is when a steer is wrestled to the ground by twisting it around by the horns. The maneuver was used on working ranches around the state, but it became even more popular when Pickett performed it as part of traveling Wild West shows.

Nowadays, famous Texans are more likely to be entertainers or athletes. Some of these people may live on ranches and own livestock. Yet, they are recognized for skills in their areas of expertise—not as rough-and-ready cowhands.

began her career as the lead singer in her family's band, Los Dinos. English was her first language, but she started singing in Spanish at the suggestion of her father. Soon, she became a successful solo artist who was well known and beloved throughout the Spanish-speaking world.

Selena had just released her first English-language album when she was shot and killed in 1995 by the former president of her Texas fan club. She was so popular in her native Texas that then-governor George W. Bush proclaimed "Selena Day" in the state two weeks after her death. A film based on Selena's life, starring Jennifer Lopez, was released in 1997.

Beyoncé Knowles is another Texas singer who goes by one name when she performs. Born in Houston, Beyoncé was part of the successful group Destiny's Child before releasing her first solo album. *Dangerously in Love* won five Grammy Awards in 2004. Recently, Beyoncé has branched out into acting, appearing in films like *The Pink Panther* and *Dreamgirls*.

The original American Idol, Kelly Clarkson first appeared in talent shows and musicals staged by her high school in Burleson.

Kelly Clarkson, from Fort Worth, won fame as the first winner on *American Idol*, in 2002. Dallas' Stevie Ray Vaughan, ranked by *Rolling Stone* magazine as one of the greatest guitarists of all time, was a rocker. In country music, which is very popular in Texas, the legendary George Strait (from Poteet) and Willie Nelson (from Abbott) have had long, extremely successful careers.

Sports Greats

Seven-time Tour de France winner Lance Armstrong was born and raised in Plano. As a professional triathlete (swimming, cycling, and running) at age sixteen, Armstrong left high school to train with

Lance Armstrong biked through Plano, Texas, as a kid. He later conquered the Paris countryside, winning the Tour de France seven times.

the U.S. Olympic cycling team. He became the nation's amateur cycling champion in 1990. Despite winning several important races, Armstrong finished poorly in two Olympic attempts (1992 and 1996), and he didn't even finish his first Tour de France in 1993.

Armstrong almost didn't get the chance to prove himself as a Tour de France contender. In 1996, he was diagnosed with testicular cancer that had spread to his lungs and brain. Doctors gave him a less than 50 percent chance of surviving. However, Armstrong beat the odds and was eventually declared cancer-free. He then joined the U.S. Postal Service cycling team and, in 1999, became only the second American to win the prestigious Tour de France. He followed that by winning the race six more times, as well as an Olympic bronze medal.

Armstrong, who lives in Austin, retired from professional cycling in 2005, in part to spend more time working on his LIVESTRONG charitable organization. However, he announced in September 2008 that he would return to the sport—and the Tour de France.

Other Texans who have made their mark as successful sports figures include two-time heavyweight boxing champion George Foreman (from Marshall) and Indy racing superstar A. J. Foyt (from Houston).

Timeline

1528	Alvar Núñez Cabeza de Vaca and crew are shipwrecked near Galveston and begin exploration.
1685	French explorer La Salle lands in Texas by mistake; establishes Fort St. Louis.
1716	The first Spanish civilian colony is established.
1821	Mexico gains independence from Spain; Stephen Fuller Austin establishes the first American colony in Texas.
1836	The Texas Declaration of Independence is adopted; battle at the Alamo; defeat of the Mexican army at San Jacinto; end of the Texas Revolution; Sam Houston is elected president.
1837	The Republic of Texas is officially recognized by the United States.
1845	United States annexes Texas, the twenty-eighth state in the Union.
1861	Texas secedes from the Union at the start of the Civil War.
1870	Texas is readmitted to the Union.
1900	The "Great Storm," the greatest natural disaster in human terms ever to strike North America, destroys much of Galveston and kills more than six thousand people.
1901	An oil gusher in Beaumont leads to the east Texas oil boom.
1953	Dwight D. Eisenhower becomes the first Texas-born president of the United States.
1963	NASA opens the Manned Spacecraft Center, later called the Lyndon Johnson Space Center, in Houston.
1988	George H. W. Bush is elected president of the United States.
2000	Former Texas governor George W. Bush wins a close race for president.
2008	Hurricane Ike, the third-most destructive storm ever in the United States, hits Texas.

State motto	"Friendship"
State capital	Austin
State flower	Bluebonnet
State bird	Mockingbird
State insect	Monarch butterfly
State fish	Guadalupe bass
State fruit	Red grapefruit
State gemstone/ mineral	Blue topaz
State nickname	The Lone Star State
State song	"Texas, Our Texas"
Statehood date and number	1845, 28
Total area and U.S. rank	268,581 square miles (695,621 sq km)
Population	23,904,380 (As of July 1, 2007)
Length of coastline	367 miles (591 km)

State Flag

State Seal

Most populated city	Houston
Highest elevation	8,749 feet (2,667 km)
Lowest elevation	Sea level
Major rivers	Rio Grande, Red River
Major lakes	Calaveras Lake, Braunig Lake, Lake Findley (Alice City Lake)
State dance	Square dance
Chief agricultural products	Cotton, corn, wheat, sorghum, rice, nursery plants
Major industries	Oil exploration and production, farming/ranching, manufacturing, banking, insurance, mining, personal services
Hottest temperature recorded	120 degrees Fahrenheit (49 degrees Celsius)
Coldest temperature recorded	-23°F (-31°C)
Origin of state name	"Texas" means "friends" in the Caddoan language of the Hasinai

State Bird

State Flower

GLOSSARY

annexation To make a territory part of a country.

brush A dry, dusty area with scraggly trees and prickly bushes.

Caddo An advanced Native American group that lived in Texas and had sophisticated farming and agricultural practices.

conservative Favoring traditional views and values.

constitution A document outlining the organization, authority, and laws of a government.

gulf A body of water formed when the ocean is partly enclosed by land.

inhospitable Not welcoming or able to sustain life.

legislator An elected official who proposes and passes laws.

liberal Open to reform and change.

manufacturing Making goods from raw materials.

mohair A type of wool made from goat hair.

Paleoamericans The early inhabitants of North and South America.

plural executive When the executive power of a state/country is divided among many individuals.

political appointment When someone is named to a specific political office.

prairie A wide swathe of land with grass and no trees.

rancher A farmer who raises livestock; in Texas, that means cows, horses, sheep, and goats.

secede To break away from an organization or, in the case of the American Civil War, a country.

subsidies Payments designed as an incentive to keep farming profitable.

subsistence farming When only enough crops to feed a farmer and his or her family are grown.

Tejano Person of Hispanic descent living in Texas.

FOR MORE INFORMATION

Bob Bullock Texas State History Museum

P.O. Box 12874

Austin, TX 78711

(512) 936-8746

Web site: http://www.thestoryoftexas.com

The museum interprets the continually unfolding story of Texas through programs and interactive exhibits. It is an invaluable resource that seeks to preserve the history of the state.

Daughters of the Republic of Texas

510 East Anderson Lane

Austin, TX 78752

(512) 339-1997

Web site: http://www.drt-inc.org

Located onsite at the Alamo, the library is dedicated to advancing the understanding of the unique history of the Alamo and Texas, and of the lives of those who experienced it.

Office of the Governor

P.O. Box 12428

Austin, TX 78711-2428

(512) 463-1782

Web site: http://www.governor.state.tx.us

The office provides news releases and continuously updated information on the state's economy, culture, safety, and prospective future.

Texas Historical Commission

1511 Colorado Street

Austin, TX 78701

(512) 463-6100

Web site: http://www.thc.state.tx.us

The Texas Historical Commission preserves Texas's architectural, archeological, and cultural landmarks.

Texas State Library and Archives Commission
1201 Brazos
P.O. Box 12927
Austin TX 78711-2927
(512) 463-5455
Web site: http://www.tsl.state.tx.us

Through programs, services, and archives, the Texas State Library provides information on the Lone Star State.

Web Sites

Due to the changing nature of Internet links, Rosen Publishing has developed an online list of Web sites related to the subject of this book. This site is updated regularly. Please use this link to access the list:

http://www.rosenlinks.com/uspp/txpp

FOR FURTHER READING

Alter, Judy. *Martin de Leon: Tejano Empresario*. Abilene, TX: State House Press, 2007.

Dodson Wade, Mary. *All Around Texas: Regions and Resources*. Portsmouth, NH: Heinemann, 2008

Gregson, Susan R. *Sam Houston: Texas Hero*. Mankato, MN: Compass Point Books, 2006.

Hanson-Harding, Alexandra. *Texas*. New York, NY: Children's Press, 2008.

Roberts, Russell. *Texas Joins the United States*. Hockessin, DE: Mitchell Lane Publishers, Inc., 2008.

Sasek, Miroslav. *This Is Texas*. New York, NY: Universe Publishing, Inc., 2006.

Stewart, Mark. *Texas Native Peoples*. Portsmouth, NH: Heinemann, 2008.

Torres, John Albert. *The Texas Fight for Independence: From the Alamo to San Jacinto*. Berkeley Heights, NJ: Enslow Publishers, 2006.

BIBLIOGRAPHY

Campbell, Randolph B. *Gone to Texas: A History of the Lone Star State*. New York, NY: Oxford University Press, Inc., 2003.

Energy Information Administration. "Coal Production." December 2007. Retrieved October 2008 (http://www.eia.doe.gov/neic/infosheets/coalproduction.html).

Fanin, Blair. "Texas Agriculture Production Sets Record at $21.8 Billion." *Southwest Farm Press*, May 2008. Retrieved October 2008 (http://southwestfarmpress.com/news/agriculture-production-0522).

Federal Reserve Bank of Dallas. "Houston Business—A Perspective on the Houston Economy." June 2005. Retrieved October 2008 (http://www.dallasfed.org/research/houston/2005/hb0504.html).

Garrison, Laura. "Rivers of Texas." *The Encyclopedia of Earth*, October 2008. Retrieved October 2008 (http://www.eoearth.org/article/Rivers_of_Texas).

Gorov, Linda. "Texas Town Makes Spanish Official, Stirs War of Words." *Boston Globe*, August 28, 1999, p. E08.

Powell, Mary Jo. *On-the-Road Histories: Texas*. Northampton, MA: Interlink Books, 2005.

Richardson, Rupert N., et. al. *Texas, the Lone Star State*. Upper Saddle River, NJ: Prentice Hall, 1997.

Rodriguez, O., E., Jaime, and Kathryn Vincent. *Myths, Misdeeds, and Misunderstandings: The Roots of Conflict in U.S.-Mexican Relations*. Lanham, MD: SR Books (Rowman & Littlefield), 1997, p. 69.

Texas Department of Agriculture. "Texas Agriculture Packs a Punch." Retrieved October 2008 (http://www.gotexan.org/gt/channel/render/items/0,1218,1670_1693_0_1692,00.html).

Texas Diary. "Famous Texas Cowboys." Retrieved November 2008 (http://www.texasdiary.com/history/famous-cowboys.html#Jack).

Toonkel, Rob. "Official English Legislation Remains Popular in Texas, Survey Finds." U.S. English, Inc., August 2008. Retrieved October 2008 (http://www.us-english.org/view/486).

University of Texas at Austin. "Texas Politics." May 2008. Retrieved November 2008 (http://texaspolitics.laits.utexas.edu).

U.S. Department of Agriculture. *Economic Research Service State Fact Sheets: Texas*, October 2008. Retrieved October 2008 (http://www.ers.usda.gov/statefacts/TX.htm).

INDEX

A

Alamo, 12, 17, 34
Alvarez de Pineda, Alonso, 13
annexation/statehood, 16, 17, 18, 20
Apache, 13
Armstrong, Lance, 37–38
Austin, 11, 12
Austin, Stephen, 15–16, 33–34

B

Beaumont, 10, 19
Big Bend region, 8, 12
Big Thicket Nature Preserve, 7
Blakely, William, 6
Bowie, Jim, 17
Bush, George H. W., 33
Bush, George W., 33, 36

C

Cabeza de Vaca, Alvar Núñez, 13–14
Caddo, 13
Civil War, 17–18, 19, 20, 24
Clarkson, Kelly, 37
coal, 29–30
Coronado, Francisco Vasquez de, 14
cowboys, 5, 36
Crockett, Davy, 17

D

Dallas, 5, 11, 12, 27

E

Eisenhower, Dwight, 33
El Paso, 11, 12
executive branch of government, 23–25

F

farming and ranching, 29, 30–31
Foreman, George, 38
Fort Worth, 11, 12
Foxx, Jamie, 34
Foyt, A. J., 38
France, 14–15

G

Galveston/Galveston Island, 5, 10, 13
Garcia, Francisco, 36
Goodnight, Charles, 36
Gulf Coast, 8, 10, 11, 14, 27, 28
Gulf of Mexico, 8, 10, 28

H

Hewitt, Jennifer Love, 35
Higgins, Pattillo, 19
Hill Country, 8
Houston, 10, 11, 27, 31, 37
Houston, Sam, 17, 34

J

Johnson, Lyndon, 33
judicial branch of government, 26

K

Kennedy, John F., 5
Knowles, Beyoncé, 37

L

La Salle, 14
legislature, 25–26
Longoria Parker, Eva, 35

Lucas, Anthony, 19
Lyndon B. Johnson Space Center, 11, 27

M

manufacturing, 31–32
McConaughey, Matthew, 35
Mexico, 8, 9, 10, 12, 14, 15–17, 24, 33

N

Nelson, Willie, 37

O

oil, 5, 10, 11, 19, 27–30
Omohundro, John Baker, 36

P

Padre Island National Seashore, 8
Paleoamericans, 13
Pickett, Bill, 36
Piney Woods, 7, 8, 27
plural executive branch, 23–24
Prairies and Lakes region, 7–8, 12
Pueblos, 13

R

Red River, 9–10
Republic of Texas, 17, 20, 34
Rio Grande, 8–9, 12, 13, 14

S

Sabine River, 9
San Antonio, 11–12, 17
San Jacinto, battle of, 17, 34
Santa Ana, 17
Selena, 35–36
slavery, 5, 17–18
South Texas Plains, 8, 11
Spain, 14, 15, 33
Strait, George, 37

T

Tejanos, 16
Texas Constitution, 20–23
Texas Panhandle, 8, 27
Texas Revolution, 12, 16, 34

V

Vaughan, Stevie Ray, 37

About the Author

Jeanne Nagle is a journalist and writer based in Rochester, New York. Among the many titles she has written for Rosen are *In the News: Living Green* and *Great Lifelong Learning Skills*. Nagle aspires to travel across America, soaking up the sights, history, and culture in all fifty states. Until then, she'll settle for in-depth research into regions that spark the imagination, beginning with Texas.

Photo Credits

Cover (top left), p. 18 Library of Congress Prints and Photographs Division; cover (top right) Wikimedia Commons, from NASA; cover (bottom) © www.istockphoto.com/ John Zellmer; pp. 3, 6, 13, 20, 27, 33, 39 © www.istockphoto.com/Rick Hyman; p. 4 (top) © GeoAtlas; pp. 7, 9 © David Muench/Corbis; p. 11 © William Manning/Corbis; p. 14 National Park Service; p. 16 Kean Collection/Hulton Archive/Getty Images; p. 21 Texas State Library & Archives Commission; p. 22 © www.istockphoto.com/David Gilder; pp. 25, 30 (bottom) Shutterstock.com; p. 28 © George Steinmetz/Corbis; p. 30 (top) © www.istockphoto.com/DHuss; p. 32 Andy Sacks/Stone/Getty Images; p. 34 The R. W. Norton Art Gallery, Shreveport, LA; p. 35 Kevin Winter/Getty Images; p. 37 Chris McGrath/Getty Images; p. 38 Franck Fife/AFP/Getty Images; p. 40 (left) Courtesy of Robesus, Inc.; pp. 40 (right), 41 (left) Wikimedia Commons; p. 41 (right) Wikimedia Commons, from the U.S. Army Corps of Engineers.

Designer: Les Kanturek; Editor: Nicholas Croce;
Photo Researcher: Cindy Reiman